AZTEC EMPIRE

A BRIEF HISTORY FROM BEGINNING TO END

HISTORY HUB

Bonus Downloads

*Get Free Books with **Any Purchase** History Shorts*

Every purchase comes with a FREE download!

or Click Here.

Aztec Empire

A Brief History from Beginning to the End

History Shorts

CONTENTS

Chapter One: Introduction

Chapter Two: The Legends of their Origin

Chapter Three: Political Struggles: The Triple Alliance

Chapter Four: The Downfall: The Spaniards

Chapter Five: Slaves

Chapter Six: Commoners (Macehualtin) & Merchants

Chapter Seven: Warriors

Chapter Eight: Nobility (Pipiltin)

Chapter Nine: Aztec Priests

Chapter Ten: King (Tlatoani)

Chapter Eleven: Gods and Goddess

Chapter Twelve: Their Mythological Beginning and the Afterlife

Chapter Thirteen: Human Sacrifice & Festivals

Chapter Fourteen: Purpose

Chapter Fifteen: Architecture and Its Symbolisms

Chapter Sixteen: Conclusion

Chapter Seventeen: Discussion Question

Chapter Eighteen: Quiz Question

Your Free Bonus Download

Chapter One
Introduction

America's history is as rich as the history of Europe. Some people sometimes forget that America has a history that does not involve the "usual" American history, like the story of the Founding Fathers. The history of America goes deeper than that. Also, America covers a wide expanse of land and history, so it will most definitely have a rich backstory. Part of the land's history is largely composed of Mesoamerica, an interesting historical region encompassing the Mayans, Aztecs, and Incan Empires. But for this study, you will be focusing on the Aztecs.

The Aztecs started as nomadic people. When they finally found a place to settle, they created the city of Tenochtitlán. However, they were not an empire just yet. They were under the rule of the Tepanecs until the Azcapotzalco came in. The Aztecs soon formed a bond with two other cities, Tepanecs and Texcoco, which birthed the Triple Alliance. They succeeded in their mission to overthrow the Azcapotzalco. However, it soon revealed that this Alliance was not a "match made in heaven." Inequality was woven into their Alliance, and they soon dispersed. But the strong Aztec leadership, which remained in their ranks in the next years, accomplished so much, from conquering different cities and forming alliances with others. However, their demise came when the Spaniards arrived and took advantage of their friendship.

Besides their history, there also is great importance in the way they lived their lives. To really know their history, you must know what it was like to be in their time and community. Their social order is similar to that of the Europeans. However, they still have very different takes on it. Their view on slavery, for example, is quite different because slaves still had rights and even benefits while the European slaves have neither. The status as a slave is also not hereditary, and so is their kingship, which is another difference between them and the Europeans. However, similarities such as nobility being hereditary are still there. You will also see that they have similar gender roles as with every culture in the world. For example, men are for outdoor work, and women are for household chores. Their education system is also gender-based.

Moreover, their religion is a big part of their everyday lives, and this manifests and guides every action they take. The Aztecs believe it is their duty to make sure the world is safe since there is not much of anything for them in the afterlife. They have gods like many other civilizations do. Their gods, while generous of earthly bounty, are also wrathful, so the Aztecs do everything in their power to ensure the gods stay pleased with them. They, like many others, still fear their gods as much as they worship them in everything they do. More interestingly, their rituals of human sacrifice are based on their creation story. The gods spilled blood to create the world and humanity, thus, they demand blood in exchange for the good fortune bestowed upon the earth.

Another awe-inspiring facet of the Aztec civilization is their art. Contrary to how art is mostly regarded today, Aztec art is not meant for admiration and mainly serves religious functions. Again, the Aztecs are unique in this aspect compared to their European counterparts. For the Europeans, art is a lavish thing, but for the Aztecs, it is something they must create to survive. For example, some of their artworks are tools meant for worship—an ornate place to leave the hearts of their sacrificed humans as a peace offering for their gods who decide to come to visit them down here on earth. In this sense, their art is reflective of their rich culture and history.

When you start this primer, you will first read about the rise and fall of the Aztec Empire, shining a light in their history, which then illuminates their culture and religion. As you read on, you will be able to connect the different aspects of their lives, and you will understand the reason behind every single development in their civilization. This will give context as to why they make human sacrifices, and why they were so accepting of the Spaniards when they first set foot on their land.

Chapter Two
The Legends of their Origin

The beginning of the Aztec Empire is not as set in stone as one would like. In their myths, the god Huitzilopochtli named them Mexica. According to legend, Aztlan, which translates to "place of the herons," is the first home of the Aztecs. Aztlan was home to seven tribes, who lived in seven separate caves. The tribes, Alcolhua, Tepanec, Xochimilca, Tlalhuica, Tlaxcalans, Chalca, and the Aztecs themselves, are collectively known as the Chichimec. They are hunter-gatherers who live very simple lives.

At one point in time, all tribes except the Aztecs left the land to create their own place and cultures. The Aztecs did not join them because they are praying for a sign from the gods to tell them to leave. After 300 years of waiting, an eagle came to them, and as this was what they were waiting for, they finally left Aztlan.

The Aztecs became nomadic, searching for home with not much luck. However, they did stay at Tula, a Toltec city, for a while. During this time, the Toltec civilization is rapidly dying. They eventually left their capital and so did the Aztecs. But they did find another abandoned city that they made a home of: Teotihuacan, known as the home of the gods (however this was built by the Olmecs). The Aztec people were fascinated with the two pyramids and the temple of the god Quetzalcoatl and were intrigued by the paintings on the walls that told the story of the first settlers in this abandoned city.

After over 100 years of being nomads, the Aztecs found a place in the Valley of Mexico where they met the tribes who used to live with them in Aztlan. The valley is big enough to keep the seven tribes, however the Aztecs were forced to set up their home in the poorest part of the land called Chapultepec, which translates to "grasshopper hill." Even though the Culhua were the primary settlers in the valley, everyone but the Aztecs had their own land rights. This made the Aztecs unwelcomed settlers, as they lived in the Valley of Mexico without the permission of the Culhua. Despite this, they stayed for 40 years.

The end of Chapultepec was brought about by an evil sorcerer named Copil who arrived in the land, thirsty for revenge and blaming the Aztecs for the death of his mother. According to the legends, he possessed dark magic that he used to create tension between the Aztecs and local chiefs. Copil created an army to attack the Aztecs, hoping that it was enough to wipe them out. However, Copil was not powerful enough. The god, Huitzilopochtli, exposed his plans to the Aztecs priests so the tribe was able to prepare their own army.

Their god instructed them to kill Copil by beheading. They also stole his heart. The chief priest brought Copil's heart to Lake Texcoco and tossed it there. But while this was happening, the Culhua invaded and killed the Aztec leader. This made them a landless tribe again. The Aztecs begged the Culhua to give them some land to live on, so they were forced to settle somewhere worse than Chapultepec: Tizapan, which was covered in volcanic rocks and home to poisonous snakes. This landscape made a livelihood through agriculture incredibly hard.

However, even though the conditions at Tizapan were not ideal, the Aztecs stayed there for almost 25 years. They were able to clear the land of its impurities and made it suitable for farming. The Culhua king was hoping the Aztecs would give up and leave to find a new home, but he was mistaken. When he found out what the Aztecs did to the land, he was surprised. Impressed, he asked the Aztecs to join in on an alliance with him, which they agreed to. With them at each other's side, they formed a revered army in all of the Valley of Mexico.

At this point, the Aztecs have immersed themselves in different cultures. They adopted their learnings from the Toltecs in Tula, and the Olmecs in Teotihuacan. They brought in Quetzalcoatl into their already long list of gods who demanded blood sacrifices for saving their tribe from the wrath of Copil and for reconciling them with the Culhua.

Chapter Three
Political Struggles: The Triple Alliance

Since the Aztecs were still under the rule of the Tepanecs, they were asked to pay tribute by serving as mercenaries or warriors. But the Tepanecs weren't tyrannical. They still gave the Aztecs some wealth as a prize for their loyalty and services. However, the system was disrupted when the Azcapotzalco people entered the picture.

Azcapotzalco's power increased, and the Aztecs and the other tribes, including the Tepanecs, were forced to pay even more tribute than usual. This caused tension between the different districts. Finally, it came to the point when the Aztecs and the Texcoco people joined forces to overthrow the Azcapotzalco. Towards the end, the Tepanecs joined in, forming the Triple Alliance, and together they overruled the Azcapotzalco.

Sadly, after the win, the Triple Alliance crumbled under disputes. The Texcoco and Aztecs received 2/5 each from the spoils of the war while the Tepanecs (from Tlacopan) only received 1/5. However, the demise of the alliance was ultimately brought about by the arrogance of the people of Tenochtitlán (the Aztecs) who cut their ties with both cities.

The first ruler of the Aztec people was Acamapichtli (1375-1395), who came into power at the age of 20 by claiming that he was a descendant of the Toltecs (the presumed beginnings of the Aztecs). He was married multiple times during his reign. He first married Ilancleitl, the daughter of the Culhuacán, for strategic purposes; after which he also married four other women from the Tenochtitlán districts. He created some of the first laws of the Aztecs and started the trend of stone houses. He also started the work on the Great Pyramid, also known as the Templo Mayor of Tenochtitlán, which was completed in the year 1487.

The next ruler was Huitzilihuitl. He married the daughter of the ruler of Azcapotzalco to whom they used to pay tribute to before the Triple Alliance. His second wife gave birth to Moctezuma I (who later would become a king as well). He paved the way for the cotton trade.

Huitzilihuitl was succeeded by Chimalpopoca, who ruled for only nine years. He was the first ruler to try and overthrow the Azcapotzalco, which led to his assassination before he could succeed. His death, however, sparked the fire in the next ruler to finally form the Triple Alliance.

The ruler who instigated the Triple Alliance was Itzcóatl. He joined forces with the rulers of Texcoco and Tlacopan (the Tepanecs) to overthrow the Azcapotzalco. They succeeded in the year 1428.

The first ruler of the Aztec Empire is Moctezuma I. He was known as a wise ruler, a fierce warrior, and a statesman who was able to conquer the city of Chalco. He documented Aztec history and started the quest to find Aztlan (where people believed Mexica came from). Even though he faced problems such as the four-year drought, he still restored order and prosperity by improving the fresh water supply and land utility. He also oversaw the construction of sculptures, temples, and botanical gardens. He also started the "Guerra Florida," which translates to "War of Flowers." This tradition is similar to when two armies choose one champion each to battle it out for the rest of the military. Warriors who died in the Guerra Florida were awarded the title "Xochimiquiztli" which means "flowery/blissful/fortunate death."

The ruler after Moctezuma I was Axayacatl, the grandson of Itzcóatl. It must have been hard to follow through after a ruler like Moctezuma I, so to prove his greatness, Axayacatl conquered Cotaxtla, and the prisoners were used as human sacrifices. He expanded the empire through war, diplomacy, and trade. He conquered Toluca, parts of Malinalco and Matlatzinca, Tuxpan. Despite his sister's marriage to the ruler of Tlatelolco, he conquered them too. Even though he focused on war, he also oversaw the creation of the grand temple of Huitzilopochtli.

Tizoc ruled after Axayacatl for five years. Although his reign was short, he conquered a lot of cities: "Tonalimoquetzayan, Toxico, Ecatepec, Cillán, Tecaxic, Tolocan, Yancuitlan, Tlappan, Atezcahuacan, Mazatlán, Xochiyetla, Tamapachco, Ecatliquapechco, and Miquetlan." He died in his sleep, though most people suspected he was poisoned.

The last Tlatoani (meaning overall ruler) of the Aztec Empire was Ahuitzotl, known to be one of the greatest military leaders in Pre-Columbian Mesoamerica. He doubled the Aztec Empire's size by conquering Zapotec, Mixtec, and many others. He also introduced the great-tailed grackle, a bird species, to the Valley of Mexico.

Chapter Four
The Downfall: The Spaniards

The Spaniards who came to the New World (which refers to the North and South of America) were called conquistadors or conquerors. They were led by the 3Gs: God, Gold and Glory. They saw the Aztecs and thought of them as uncivilized and religiously astray. They believed that the only one to worship is Jesus Christ and their mission is to convert these pagan Aztecs. Besides that, the Spaniards believed that, as a reward for their hard work, the gold and other treasures of the Aztecs were theirs.

The interest of the Spaniards in the Valley of Mexico started with Juan de Grijalva. From Cuba, he went west, travelling to the coast of Mexico where he found a village that gave his delegation treasures. de Grijalva brought these back to Diego Velásquez de Cuéllar, the governor of Cuba then. He was delighted with the gifts and wanted more, so he sent representatives to the Yucatan Peninsula, which is southeast of Mexico. This land was inhabited by the Mayans.

In 1518, Velásquez gave Hernan Cortés permission to embark on a three-ship expedition to the Yucatan Peninsula, with the goal of bringing home more wealth. In the end, Cortés brought 11 ships, 500 men and horses, with enough provisions for everyone.

Because of his immense force and resources, Cortés went beyond Velásquez's original plans, which was to explore and check for possible future trips. Now that Cortés did more than expected, Velásquez was afraid that Cortés would try to overthrow him. Alarmed, he ordered Cortés to stop his expedition and step down. Cortés did not listen, and continued his voyage, passing the posts of Trinidad and Havana, on his way to Mexico.

When word got out that there were Spaniards who had landed in Mexico, Moctezuma II was intrigued and sent messengers to meet with Cortés in Totonacapan. Moctezuma II's delegation was ordered to greet the Spaniards with open arms and even brought him goods and gifts, including a serpent mask inlaid with turquoise, a garment made of feathers, necklaces of shells and other items made of gold.

Cortés pretended to be nice to them at first. That is, until he made his men ride to the Aztec Empire with swords and ammunition of gunpowder (which scared the Aztecs even more because they had never heard of it before). He said that the Aztecs should prepare for a hand-to-hand combat as a test. Cortés provided the Aztec messengers with swords, spears, and leather shields.

The messengers were baffled. They did not know what to do; they were nice, followed the rules and the orders of their ruler. They expected kindness but were greeted with hostility. So, when the messengers got back to Tenochtitlan, they reported everything that had happened, every single detail, from the gunpowder to the Spanish armor and horses. The Aztecs have never seen horses until that time.

Moctezuma II believed in his army and that they were great enough to match the Spaniards, so he didn't fear the threat of an invasion. However, he did want to gain more knowledge of these invaders, so he sent more men to the Spaniards. This time, instead of simple messengers, he sent warriors and prophets. He also sent some captives to be sacrificed just in case these Spaniards are reincarnations of their gods. When the Spaniards witnessed the captives being sacrificed, they were horrified. When they refused this, the Aztecs then knew that these Spaniards were no god of theirs.

Because of the Totonacs, Cortés knew about Tenochtitlan and its treasures. As they went on, they encountered the Otomi in battle. Because of their rituals before battle, the Otomi were overpowered. The Spaniards did not have the same customs and charged as soon as the battle began. The Otomi were slaughtered and the news of their defeat spread quickly.

When the Spaniards crossed paths with Tlaxcalans, they found another ally. With the news of the Otomi's great army's demise, the Tlaxcalans did not want to suffer the same fate. Hence, the Tlaxcalans joined forces with them, offering their manpower and intelligence about Tenochtitlan. The Spaniards pressed on, defeating the Cholultecas as well.

The Aztecs tried their best to stop the invasion, offering the Spaniards plenty of gifts, which just motivated the conquerors to charge on. When the Spaniards finally arrived at the Aztec Empire's capital city, Tenochtitlan, they were ready for war. Their numbers reached thousands, and they got the intel they needed.

Moctezuma II went out to meet the Spaniards at the entrance of the city and approached Cortés with the Aztec polite welcome. However, Cortés abused their civility and took this diplomatic action as a form of surrender.

Cortés asked to see the Aztec gods and to be introduced to their religion. While the Aztecs saw their religion as fair, Cortés was disgusted by all the blood. He did not understand them so he asked if they could have a Christian cross placed in the Aztec temple. This request offended them all.

Moctezuma II eventually came under orders of Cortés. The presence of Spanish culture in his city slowly made Moctezuma II revert his ways, and the king started to trust the invaders. So when Moctezuma II let them into the treasury, the Spaniards took every single treasure and burned everything else. Now that they have momentum, Cortés made a subtle plan to fully take on the city. He planned to make Moctezuma II a prisoner in his own home and use him as a puppet. However, it was futile because when the Aztecs realized this, they stopped being docile.

Meanwhile, because of the brewing feud between Velásquez and Cortés, the Governor sent troops to arrest Cortés. Cortés took as many soldiers with him to meet Velásquez's forces at the coast. This gave the Aztec people the chance to take their empire back, which they did successfully.

However, Cortés was persistent. He went back and took control of Tenochtitlan. He also wanted revenge for all his men who died when the Aztecs took back their city. But this time, the Spaniards didn't only bring troops, they also brought tools for biological warfare to which the Aztecs succumbed to. They had no means to fight a pandemic and a war at the same time.

When Tenochtitlan fell, so did the Aztec Empire.

This is an Aztec building in Mexico.

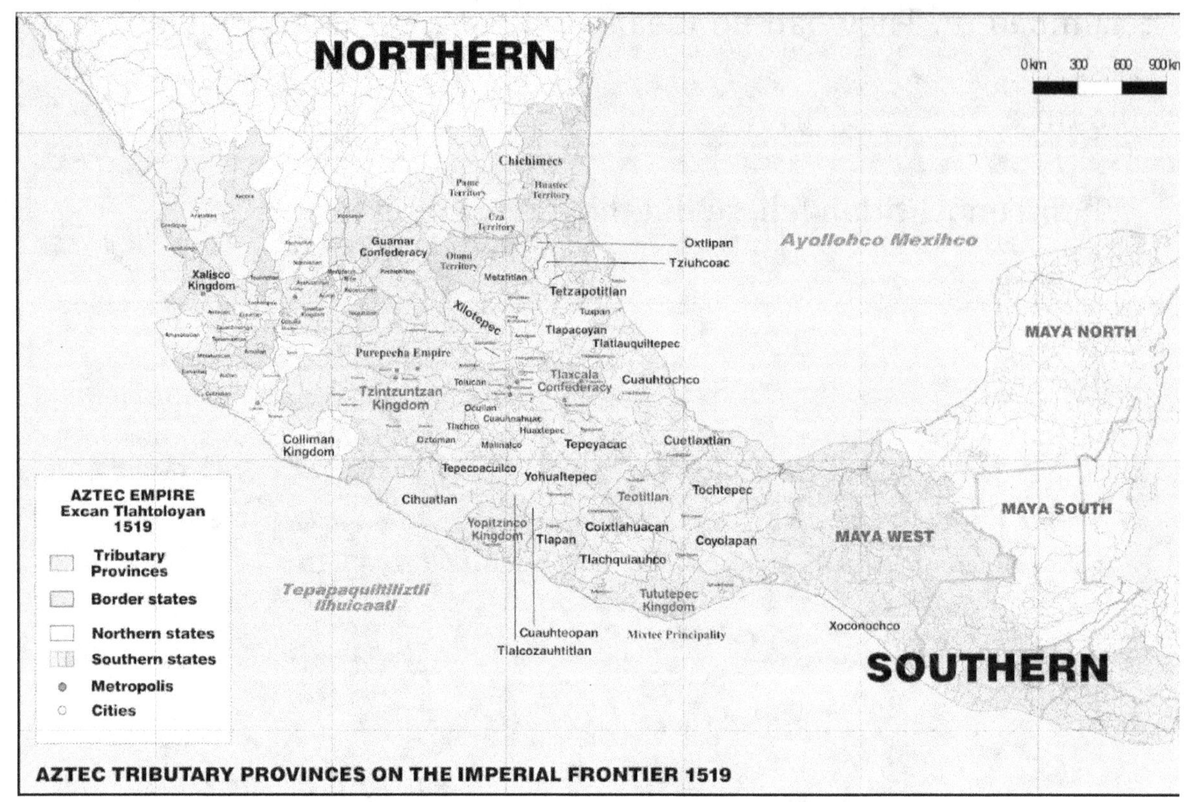

This is the map of the Aztec Empire.

Chapter Five
Slaves

The slaves in the Aztec Empire were in the lowest social class. Anyone could become a slave if they were in debt (from gambling or other reasons), or as a form of punishment for their crimes. Some cities also use their war prisoners as slaves. However, there were even people who chose to become slaves because the Aztecs believed they should live their lives however they wanted to.

While stealing and selling children as slaves were illegal, slaves were sold and bought in a specific market. One could only hope to get a good master who would keep them fed, clothed, and sheltered. The worst that could happen is if a slave was sold to a Priest. That would mean they would be sacrificed to the gods. The slave market was strictly regulated so that no crimes were committed during trades or sales.

However, Aztec slaves were different from the slaves in Europe or in America. First, slaves in the Aztec Empire were allowed to have their own property, meaning they had their own clothes, could buy land, had money, and even had the freedom to buy their own slaves as their assistants. They were also free to marry one woman. Apparently, it was normal for a woman owner to marry a slave if they become a widow. Also, if they had children, they weren't restricted to being a slave as well, as slavery was not inherited. But most importantly, slaves weren't outcasts in the Aztec Empire. They weren't required to pay taxes and serve in the military because their sole purpose was to serve their master.

However, even though slavery in the Aztec Empire seemed good because of their slaves' rights and privileges, they were not seen as citizens. They were still regarded as properties, as objects to be bought and sold.

Chapter Six
Commoners (Macehualtin) & Merchants

Commoners, composed of farmers and craftsmen, were the most populated social class in the Aztec Empire. They were also soldiers, but all Aztec men were warriors at their core. Women in this social class had the usual jobs: cleaning, cooking, staying at home, taking care of children, and the like.

Young boys were expected to go to school once they reach the age of five. Schools for commoners were called telpochcalli. Here, they were taught to sing, dance, and play musical instruments. Boys were also trained to be part of the military. Like in the Korean Peninsula, men are obligated to serve in the military at a specific age.

Children in this class were motivated by fear. Parents would hit them when they did something wrong.

Marrying at the age of 12 was not uncommon in the Aztec Empire. Gender roles were very evident at that time. Men would do the hard outdoor labor while women stayed home and did household chores. Commoners were required to pay taxes and tribute, unlike the slaves. In exchange for their work, they were allowed to vote for the next chief of their district. They owned land as a group and were ruled by chiefs (calpulli).

As they owned land, they were required to make sure it was kept properly. They must continue to work on the land, and if it becomes idle for two years, they would be punished as the calpulli would see fit. However, this scenario wasn't common.

As time went on, changes happened in the way commoners lived. The nobility would eventually control the district, as the calpulli influence waned. This resulted in the commoners losing their usual share of the produce yielded from their land because they started to pay tribute to the nobility. If they couldn't pay, they pay through services (however, they aren't slaves).

The social class of merchants was created because of the expansion of the Aztec Empire. They helped transport goods from one district or city to the other. As a difference between nobility and commoners, the merchants were free to use their money as they pleased. They had more freedom than commoners but had a less lavish lifestyle compared to the nobility. They were a relatively smaller group compared to the other classes; therefore, they did not pose a threat to the upper classes. In fact, there were only twelve merchants in Tenochtitlán.

Merchants traded goods, weapons, and other things to different classes as well as different districts or cities. Like the commoners, this social class was hereditary. They also had a responsibility to the empire. They monitored the markets they worked in and were the peacemakers when fights broke out in the market.

Are You Enjoying Reading?

As an independent publisher

with a tiny marketing budget

we rely on readers, like you.

Click here to a brief review on Amazon

If you're receiving help from this book,

would you please take a moment to write a brief review?

We really appreciate it.

Chapter Seven
Warriors

For the Aztec men, being a warrior was everything. They begin their training at a very young age. Since the Aztecs didn't really have a permanent army, they did have a full range of professional officers, the leading commander being the Tlatoani. All healthy men at the age of 17 were expected to fight when the need arises.

They were trained to be well versed in different types of weapons such as spears, slings, bows and arrows, darts and dart-throwers, knives and swords. The army is divided into small groups of 200 men; these are what we now call platoons.

Their goal in a war was not the destruction of the other army but rather to expand territories and to capture war criminals. They specifically aimed to maim and not to kill. Every 11th month of each year, the tlatoani gave military honors and awards to men who deserved them.

Chapter Eight
Nobility (Pipiltin)

The nobility consisted of only five percent of the entire Aztec Empire population. To become a noble is to be born into the family, meaning it is heredity, just like the status of merchants and commoners. If a noble married a commoner, that would automatically make their children part of the nobility. They had their own schools, and although the boys were separated from the girls, they still studied religion, art, math, public speaking, and the like. They were also taught about blood sacrifices. The difference between their education was that the boys were trained in combat, as all men in the Aztec Empire.

Despite their privileges, they also had their responsibilities. They were expected to work, achieve success, and were given high-ranking positions in the government and in the military. Thus they were expected to be society's role models.

The nobles saw the commoners as their own people. They were like secondary kings, receiving tribute from their own people. They also lived in lavish palaces compared to the commoners who work in their district.

And since they were polygamous, they would often build separate houses for each of their wives.

But, as you can see, the nobility depended on the commoners to keep their positions. Since the commoners worked for them on their land, they produced goods that the nobility used to gain money. To make sure they stayed in power, they gave speeches on how important the work of commoners is. They provide them with reassurance and high praise as a reward for their hard work. And for commoners, that was enough. The nobility's last act to appease the commoners (or to prevent them from ever revolting) was to make the separation between their classes as evident as possible. These three ways were enough to keep a peaceful relationship between commoners and nobility.

Chapter Nine

Aztec Priests

Next in the social ladder were the Aztec Priests. There were two high priests and several priests under their command (they are at the same level as military leaders). The main responsibility of the high priests was to keep the gods happy and guide the people to actions that would keep the gods satisfied.

Priests had many roles when it came to the temples, overseeing everything that happened inside. They would lead the sacrifices and some were teachers. The most revered priests were the ones who worked in the Great Temple. Also, priests could serve in the military.

The lower ranking priests were from the ranks of the commoners who served the higher priests. Women could become priestesses as well, as it was not an exclusively male position.

Chapter Ten
King (Tlatoani)

Each city state had their own king. They were the commander-in-chief of the military as well as the high priest of their religion. They had the power over their people and thus were responsible for them. They were always relatives of the Aztec Royal family, which could be extensive since the Aztec king could have multiple wives.

The selection of the Tlatoani depended on the council of elders (which were all nobles). They would choose from four candidates who, most, if not all, were close relatives of the previous Tlatoani. They were compared against each other, with the elders checking who had the greatest wit, and the most courage when it came to battle. This showed that being a king was not hereditary, as the title wasn't passed on from father to son. Thus, no dynasties were formed. However, when one is chosen as the king of the capital city of Tenochtitlan, they are Tlatoani for life, from the start of their coronation to the day of their death.

This is an image of a female Aztec nobility.

This is an image of an Aztec slave with an invader.

Chapter Eleven

Gods and Goddess

The Aztecs have many gods, with each one somewhat overlapping with the other. Their society was dominated by their religion since each action they make is to appease the gods. This section will introduce the important Aztec gods as stated in the book *Aztec History: A Captivating Guide to the Aztec Empire, Mythology, and Civilization.*

Quetzalcóatl was the god of vegetation, earth and water who created life on earth. He was also the patron of Aztec priests, the inventor of books and calendars, and protector of craftsmen. He was believed to be the god who brought about the rise and fall of the Aztec civilization. At the beginning, back in the days of the Toltecs,, he was the Priest-King of Tula (their land). At first, he didn't require human sacrifices. Instead, he wanted animals such as snakes, birds, and butterflies. He was then banished from Tula by another Toltec god, Tezcatlipoca. Quetzalcóatl used his banishment as an opportunity to explore the world, crossing the Atlantic Ocean. Then he killed himself but rose from the dead and ascended into Venus's planet. He had a role in the demise of the Aztecs who thought that Hernan Cortés was his reincarnation. Believing that Quetzalcóatl had returned from his banishment, Moctezuma II and the Aztecs welcomed the Spaniards with open arms…Which was a mistake.

Huitzilopochtli was the god of the sun and war. The Aztecs believed that warriors who died in war would come back as hummingbirds. Thus, Huitzilopochtli was depicted as a hummingbird in Aztec art. He was also woven into the history of Aztecs as the god who guided the men who left to find Aztlan and led them to their great city Tenochtitlán.

Human sacrifices were most important to this god since he is the sun god, and the Aztecs worshipped the sun above all because of their creation story. They offered their sacrifice to Huitzilopochtli every day, believing that if he wasn't appeased, the world's fate would meet catastrophe and annihilation.

Tlaloc was the god of rain. His name translates to "he who makes things sprout." He was usually depicted as a man with a mask, big eyes, and fangs, and shared some similarities with the Mayan rain god, Chac. Tlaloc is important because he could help the Aztec people's crops grow and thrive, but when he was in a bad mood, he could destroy their lands, bringing on droughts, storms, hurricanes, and other natural disasters relating to water. He was also associated with diseases such as dizziness and leprosy.

Chalchiuhtlicue was the wife of Tlaloc, making her an important goddess. She was the goddess of freshwater bodies who ruled the past earth, the one before the present.

Coatlicue, the mother goddess, was the goddess of the earth, closest to the Lord and Lady of Duality. She was usually depicted as someone with two snakes on her face, with her skirt decorated with snakes as well. Since she was a mother, she also had big breasts, with her neck adorned by a necklace of bones (hands and skulls), and human hearts, which signified that the earth eats all dead things.

Chapter Twelve

Their Mythological Beginning and the Afterlife

The Aztecs believed that there were four worlds that had been destroyed before the gods created the one, we are currently in. These worlds were called Suns, and each sun was linked with one of the four main elements: earth, wind, fire, or water. The First Sun was called Four Jaguar, representing Tezcatlipoca who was usually portrayed as a jaguar. In this world, the Aztecs believed that people living on it were giants who were strong enough to pull out trees with their bare hands. This specific Sun lasted for 676 years until it was destroyed.

The Second Sun, named Nahui Ehecatl (or Four Wind), was ruled by Quetzalcoatl (the plumed serpent). This world, where humans could transform into monkeys who lived off acorns, only lasted for 364 years. It ended because the gods destroyed it with hurricanes and other wind storms.

The Third Sun was Nahui Quiahuitl or Four Rain. Tlaloc was the ruler of this Sun where people would feed on seeds and could turn into dogs and turkeys. This world was destroyed in volcanic fire.

The Fourth Sun, and the last before the current world, was ruled by Tlaloc's wife and sister, Chalchiuhtlicue. The name given to this Sun is Nahui Atl, or Four Water where the main inhabitants were fish. It lasted for only 52 years, and was destroyed by floods.

The current and Fifth Sun called Nahui Ollin, or Four Motion, was created by Tonatuih, the sun god. He was associated with Huitzilopochtli because of this.

According to the Aztec version of the Origin of Human Life, by the end of the Fourth Sun, the gods made a trip to the underworld to get the bones of their ancestors. Quetzalcoatl was chosen to travel to the ninth layer of the underworld to retrieve the bones. However, Lord Mictlan, who was often perceived as a skeleton with a conical hat, presented him with a series of tests before he could proceed with his mission.

The first test was for him to travel around the underworld four times while creating noise with a shell horn. Then Lord Mictlan tricked

Quetzalcoatl into falling into a pit to prevent him from getting the bones. Despite Lord Mictlan's mischievous tricks, Quetzalcoatl did succeed, but as he was travelling back, he accidentally dropped the bones and they broke into pieces. He still took the bones back and the gods poured blood over it, creating human life.

The Aztecs have two superior gods: Ometecuhtli (the Lord of Duality) and Omecihuatl (the Lady of Duality) who existed in the highest heaven, the 13th heaven. While they did not have a strong hand on what happened on earth, they were responsible for creation and death. The gods discussed earlier were the descendants of the Lord and Lady of Duality.

According to Aztec religion, the gods came together at twilight, and a god threw himself into the fire, turning him into the Sun. However, he couldn't move, so the other gods gave him some blood to save him.

The Aztecs believed that when someone died of leprosy, dropsy, gout, or any lung disease, they would go to Tlaloc's old paradise because he was the reason for the end of their lives on earth. So, depending on the god who had a hand in their deaths, the people would go to different paradises.

Warriors who died in battle, human sacrifices, merchants killed in distant places, and women who died from their first childbirth were said to go to paradise. The rest are sent to Mictlan, the land of nine hells where they would travel throughout the different hells and, once done, would disappear.

Chapter Thirteen

Human Sacrifice & Festivals

Human and blood sacrifices were all interwoven into the religion of the Aztec Empire. From the creation story, blood was what kept the world alive. It started with the gods giving their blood to help one another. The Aztecs believed that blood was what kept the earth moving, shielding them from annihilation. Since they didn't really have a set afterlife, they thought it was their sole duty to the world to keep it going.

For the Sun Gods, they sacrificed soldiers who they believed already secured a place in paradise. However, they did not limit themselves to just warriors. They could still find people who have the same characteristics. Aztec people were honored to be chosen for the sacrifice, because they deemed it as a privilege.

One could be sacrificed for the greater good in different ways. One is where the human sacrifice would be tied to a circular stone, leaving their body exposed, and the priests would slash his chest and take the person's heart out. Another form is similar to what the Romans did for sport and entertainment (Gladiators). The Aztecs would slow down the victim by tying a rock to their leg. They would arm them with a wooden weapon and would have them fight against an Aztec soldier wielding a real weapon and with nothing weighing them down. There was also a ritual where women would dance, and someone would cut off their heads as they did so. To appease Tlalco, the Aztecs would drown children. And for the fire god, they would throw victims into flames. For the Xipe Totec, the victims would be tied down and killed by arrows.

Human sacrifices go together with festivals done in honor of a god. Here is a list of festivals that the Aztecs celebrated:

- Atlcahualo was a festival for Tlaloque and Ehecatl. The people sacrificed in this festival were children.

- Tlacaxipehualiztli was a festival for Xipe Totec, Huitzilopochtli and Mayahuel. The victims of these were war prisoners, god impersonators, and slaves. In this festival, they killed their sacrifices by extracting their heart and flaying their skin.

- Tozoztontli was a festival for Tlaloc, Chalchiuhtlicue and Coatlicue. This was another festival that used heart extraction as the way to sacrifice their victims.

- Huey Tozoztli was a festival for Centeotl, Chicomecoatl, Quetzalcoatl and Tlaloc. The ritual started at sunrise to noon. The victims included the boys, girls and deity representatives.

- Toxcatl: The patron gods of this festival are Huitzilopochtli, Tlacahuepan, Tezcatlipoca, and Cuexcotzin. The victims included war criminals, who would get their hearts taken out of them.

- Etzalcualiztli was a festival for Quetzalcoatl and Tlaloc. Again, heart extraction was the type of sacrifice they did. However, this one was done at midnight at the shrine of Tlaloc in the Great Temple.

- Teotleco was a festival dedicated to all gods, especially Xochiquetzal. Heart extraction was their method of sacrifice.

- Quecholli: This festival's patrons are Mixcoatl, Tlamatzincatl, Izquitecatl, and Coatlicue. They extracted the heart of their victims and decapitated them. This was done usually during the day.

- Panquetzaliztli: This festival was for Huitzilopochtli. The victims were slaves and prisoners. The kind of sacrifice they did was heart extraction at the Great Temple (at the shrine of Huitzilopochtli).

This is a sculpture of Xiuhtecuhtli, the god of fire.

This is a wall painting of Quetzalcoatl.

Chapter Fourteen

Purpose

The Aztecs' actions were all based on their religion. So, it was natural that Aztec art reflected their admiration and appreciation for the gods. Their art fulfilled religious purposes and was not for personal expression. Through symbols and metaphors, they described their ways of worship and documented abstract stories of life and death, their dreams and stories that were passed down to them for generations. They made art for their gods to ensure they were appeased and believed that doing this gave power to their empire.

Initially, the Aztecs did not have any iron or bronze equipment and used bones, wood, and stone to create their art. The stones they usually used were obsidian and chert. The Aztecs focused mostly on stone carvings, and pictographs which represented words, ideas and sounds. The most common pictographs were jaguars, snakes, beetles, lightning, and wind.

Chapter Fifteen

Architecture and Its Symbolisms

Like their art, Aztec architecture reflected the value and civilization of their empire. Delving into the study of architecture will help understand the history of the Aztecs more. Tenochtitlan, present-day Mexico City, was the capital city of the Aztec Empire. Back then, it was one of the largest cities in the world. Tenochtitlan is where most of Aztec architecture could be best investigated. However, even if Tenochtitlan was the best city of the Aztec Empire, there are still other places where Aztec architecture could be studied. One of the most memorable structures in the Aztec Empire was the Great Temple where the people worshipped Huitzilopochtli and Tlaloc. Human sacrifices were done in this building to appease them.

Aztec architecture was greatly based on the Toltecs of Colhuacan, the Tepanecs of Azcapotzalco and Acolhua of Texcoco. This is so because on the quest of finding a territory to build their city in, they found these kingdoms and settled there for a while. Their architecture focused on order and symmetry, and geometric designs were greatly featured in their buildings. These patterns were rich in symbolism, mostly representing the four directions, or four corners of the earth (North, South, East and West). North was represented by the color black and was for Tezcatlipoca the god of fate, destiny and the night. North was what they called Mictlampa (which means "place of death"). It was also associated with a flint knife. South was represented by Huitzilopochtli, and the color blue. The region, called Huitzilapa, was the place of thorns and was represented by the rabbit. The East was associated with the color red and was ruled by Tonatiuh, Xipe Totec and Camaxtli-Mixcoatl. They called this region Tlapallan, meaning "place of red color." They also called it Tlapcopa, which meant "place of light" The East is symbolized by the reed. And lastly, the West, ruled by Quetzalcoatl, was represented by the color white. The West is where the sun sets, and the region was called Cihuatlampa (meaning "place of the women"). Each of the gods that represented the different corners of the world were responsible for fire, sunlight, water, earth, humanity, the dead, and time. They were in charge of the balance of the universe and of earth.

Tenochtitlan had structures that followed cosmological patterns. The Aztec people focused on keeping the balance of the world and making sure the gods approved of their actions. Otherwise, the world would be destroyed just like the previous earths (also known as Suns).

This is photo of an Ocelotl-Cuauhxicalli statue,

This is a Sun Stone.

Chapter Sixteen
Conclusion

Now that you've read everything, do you now realize how everything is intertwined with each other? History is not plainly the rise and fall of a great civilization. If you were to only focus on dates and events, you would not be able to understand the Aztecs' motives, which is far more important, or else their actions seem heartless, ignorant, and possibly even asinine (pertaining to their friendly nature towards the Spaniards). Everything is connected. Remember this.

Besides this, you must now see the difference between their ways compared to that of the Europeans. Diversity is always good because it helps you see different sides, interpretations, and perspectives. Why is this important? Simply because everything is not one-sided, including history, no matter how factual it must be. Stories always have different variations; the number depends on how many people are included in them. So, to see the similarities and differences between two cultures is something you should always take into account.

Also, we must bear in mind to learn from our history. The Aztecs made mistakes, as we all do, and their mistakes cost them their glory. Their demise, however noble their actions were, was because they were blinded by their religion. Religion is a good thing; faith is one of the things that keeps all of us going. But we must also question the actions of others. In other words: "Read the room." If the Aztecs had just realized the hostility the Spaniards were bringing to their land, if they had just opened their eyes to see how the other cities were joining forces against the Spaniards to overthrow them, they might have been able to fight back and keep their civilization.

So, the three key takeaways from reading this are that you must remember that everything is connected because that will help you have a deeper understanding of the actions and reasoning of others. This allows you to develop empathy. Two, you must always consider the different sides and take on everything because it will remind you to see everyone else's point of view; why they act the way they do. This will help you be analytical and practical. And finally, you must always learn from the past, so you do not allow history to repeat itself. No one wants war or another catastrophe to befall us.

Remember all these takeaways and lessons so you can be more understanding, considerate, practical, and analytical. These qualities are important to possess because they balance out your heart and brain, and help you become the best version of yourself. Balance is important. It keeps us both grounded and ambitious. Imagine the Yin and Yang: balance is what helps keep us human and what the world strives to become. It's something history has been trying to teach mankind for years. The perfect balance between empathy and practicality is something we all have to strive for.

Chapter Seventeen

Discussion Question

The Triple Alliance was forged because the cities were oppressed by the current system. However, there was still injustice within its agreement. Do you think inequality will always be there no matter what the circumstances? Even in circumstances as mundane as the dynamics in your friend group?

Discussion Question

The Spaniards invaded the Aztec Empire, using their friendship as a catapult to seize their wealth and land. If you were one of the Spaniards and witnessed the kindness of the Aztec people, would you still invade them for the mission? Or would you put aside the goal of your expedition and just work with the Aztecs?

Discussion Question

In Aztec culture, slavery isn't hereditary. What about this way of living say about the Aztecs? Do you think that our "house help" culture is based on the Aztec culture of slavery? Why?

Discussion Question

Nobility in the Aztec culture was passed down from generation to generation. This is similar to other cultures. Why do you think this way pervaded across other civilizations?

Discussion Question

The Aztecs believed that most people would go to hell, not because of bad deeds but because they weren't chosen to go to paradise. When they die, they thought that they will walk to the edge of hell and then disappear from existence. What would you do if this was your way of thinking? How will you live your life?

Discussion Question

The Aztecs believed the earth called for blood for it to keep living. If you were to be sacrificed, would you allow them to? Remember to take into account that in this scenario, you are part of the Aztec community.

Discussion Question

Art in the Aztec Empire fulfilled religious purposes. But art is all about the stories it holds. With this in mind, do you still call what they've made art?

Discussion Question

Aztec craftsmen made art for the gods. If you were a craftsmen, which god would you choose to honor with a sculpture? Why would you choose that god?

Chapter Eighteen
Quiz Question

1. **True/False:** The Aztecs were a nomadic clan before settling down in the Valley of Mexico. They created their city of Tenochtitlán. However, they were under the Tepanecs at first.

2. **True/False:** The Spaniards were led by Hernan Cortés who guided them to the Aztec Empire. They were gifted with gold by the Aztec pe

3. **True/False:** Merchants were the social class that came between the commoners and nobility. Because of this, they were hard workers and lavishly clothed. They were basically a mix of the best of both worlds.

4. **True/False:** To be a king, you must be elected by the Nobility. Kingship in the Aztec Empire was not hereditary at all. It was more of a democracy (but not quite) than a monarchy.

5. **True/ False:** The creation story stated that there were five Suns before our current one. The gods would usually end the world once

they find no future for it anymore. This current world we are in is the Sixth Sun.

6. **True/False:** Human sacrifices are essential for the Aztecs as a way to appease the gods. They believed it was part of their duty to keep the world turning, and to do that, they must give blood to the earth. If they didn't, they feared the gods would see no future for this earth anymore.

7. **True/False:** The Sun Stone is an example of an Aztec Sculpture made from stone. It is actually a monumental stone sculpture. It is meant to celebrate creation.

8. **True/ False:** Aztec art was meant to tell a story. It is to be admired and interpreted. They were made to keep the legacy of the Aztec Empire alive.

Quiz Answer

1. True

2. False. The Spaniards were looking for gold. Therefore, when the Aztecs kept giving them gold, their greed motivated them to conquer the Aztec Empire.

3. False. The merchants did not care for lavish clothing.

4. True

5. False. This is just the Fifth Sun.

6. . True

7. True

8. False. Aztec art is for religious and practical purposes.

Bonus Downloads

*Get Free Books with **<u>Any Purchase</u>** History Shorts*

Every purchase comes with a FREE download!

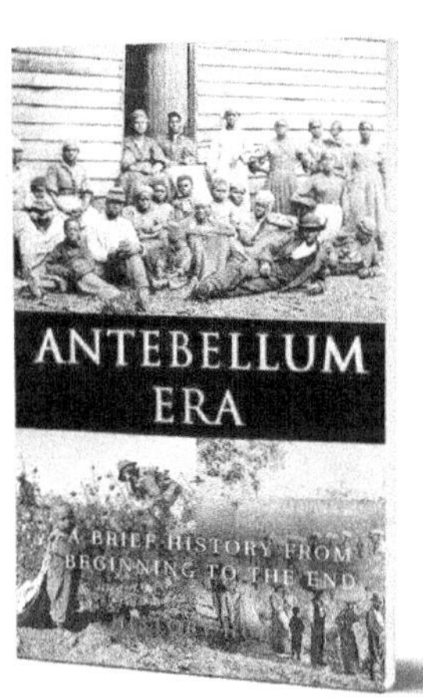

[or Click Here.](#)